Thoughts

FROM THE BOTTOM OF A

CHILI

Bowl

Thoughts

FROM THE BOTTOM OF A

CHILI Bowl

F R A N K

V A R A L L O

THOMAS NELSON PUBLISHERS
Nashville • Atlanta • London • Vancouver

Published in Nashville, Tennessee, by Thomas Nelson, Inc.

Library of Congress Cataloging-in-Publication Data

Varallo, Frank.
    Thoughts from the bottom of a chili bowl / Frank Varallo.
      p.   cm.
    ISBN 0-7852-8045-6
    1. Aphorisms and apothegms.   I. Title.
PN6271.V35   1994
818'.02—dc20   94-25836
                                                        CIP

Printed in the United States of America
1 2 3 4 5 6 7 — 00 99 98 97 96 95 94

The quotations of folk wisdom in this book have been collected over a long period of time and printed on the Varallo's Restaurant daily specials menu. Although we do not know which individuals to thank for which "thoughts," we do know that all these sayings came from the many patrons of Varallo's who so graciously over the years gave us a "thought for the day" to use. We wish to thank those people from the bottom of our hearts!

Frank and Eva Varallo

Varallo's restaurant at the 811 Church Street location

My times are in Thy hands
Grow old along with me,
The best is yet to be . . .

Robert Browning

Dedication

To our daughter Marie Eugenia Varallo, who first
envisioned the thoughts for the day on our menus
and who contributed the first one

And to our patrons, who have offered these thoughts
day after day

Today's Specials

Introduction   xi

Horse Sense & Chestnuts   1

Do's & Don't's   29

Workin' & Winnin'   59

Courtin' & Kin   103

Friends & Grins   115

Politics & Pocketbooks   137

Gettin' Old & Gettin' Good   153

Frank Varallo, Sr., violin virtuoso, Ellis Island interpreter, and founder of Varallo's restaurant

Introduction

At Varallo's Restaurant, we are known for a lot of things. We're the oldest family-owned restaurant in Nashville—we've been open almost 87 years right downtown. We specialize in chili and tamales. And we're probably the only place that allows you to substitute our homemade banana pudding for one vegetable on your vegetable plate (on Tuesdays, that is). But we're also known for our "Tho't for the Day."

It was our daughter Marie Eugenia who had a collection of thoughts for the day and started putting them on our menu. Pretty soon, the customers started contributing too. A customer comes in our restaurant and writes down a thought. Each day we choose one to print on the daily specials menu. Then we'll call the person and say, "We've used your thought for today, so you're entitled to a free chili at Varallo's." And, of course, they come in and get a free chili. Over the years customers have left us thousands of quotations. Some of them we wouldn't dare put on our menu!

But we get a lot of good quotes, and that's what gave us the idea to put some of them in a book. I enjoy reading books with quotes in them; I have several. I have a lot of quotes in my head, too, that are sayings from my father: "Help everybody you can in any way you can . . . but don't tell anybody everything you know." That's my favorite.

My father and several other restaurant men in Nashville all came from the same village—Viggiano, Italy. My father left home when he was nine years old and traveled all over the world on steamships playing the violin with orchestras and tap dancing. I loved to hear him tell me about all the places he'd been. He spoke several different languages fluently, and the first job he had in this country was as an interpreter for immigrants at Staten Island. Years later in the restaurant, he enjoyed people coming in speaking different languages. He'd sit right down and talk to them.

I was the youngest child of seven, the only one of my parents' children to be born in America. As a boy I worked in the restaurant making tamales. We used to get cornshucks out of the panhandle in Texas. We made tamales, sometimes two or three thousand a day. We had to roll them by hand, and that's how they got me in the business at nine years old. I've been here ever since.

If you come into Varallo's, you'll see the walls are full of photographs. I made a lot of those myself; developed them too. A fellow came to work for me when I was about seventeen years old, and he had some experience in photography. He saw these pictures I had made with a Graphflex, one of those cameras you look down in. He said, "Why don't you try developing those yourself?" I told him I didn't know anything about it. He said, "I can show you what little I know about it."

So he got some developer and what have you and we closed up a little room in the back of the restaurant where I did my bookkeeping. We put a light in there and started developing our own pictures. Then I fixed a little dark room in the basement at home, in what was originally a wine cellar. I was a natural for enjoying photography, I suppose. I'd gone to art school for a while as a teenager, but it got to be too expensive. Plus, first time somebody wouldn't show up to work, I couldn't go off to school because I would have to work. Photography's been my hobby ever since I learned how to develop my own pictures.

I met my wife, Eva, at a family get-together where she was doing the Charleston. In those days she was trying to make up her mind whether to become a nun, and she married me instead! We've been married 57 years. Today Eva and I still run the restaurant, and we have a ball doing it. God has blessed us greatly. We've been coaching our grandsons, Todd and Tony, teaching them what we know about the business, and they've just about taken over the restaurant. So it will still be family owned after Eva and I retire.

We do miss the old days in some ways. We've seen downtown Nashville change, especially after the war when the theaters moved out to malls. We're only open days now, and we're plenty busy. But the night business we used to have, you can't believe. People would be lined up at three in the morning. People would come in after the dances, after the games. Years ago the Princess Theater was a vaudeville house, and we'd get a lot of that night crowd, including the performers. This is what we miss most. But we can't complain; we wouldn't be able to work those kind of hours anymore anyhow.

We've had our share of celebrities—Grandpa Jones, Brenda Lee, Roy Orbison, the governor. Pat Boone and his folks come in—Pat loves our chili. We send him chili out in California. He calls us and tells us what he wants. We put the chili in plastic cottage cheese containers, freeze it, and send it to him.

The day we'd been open 75 years, a couple came in right at lunch time. They said, "We're celebrating our 50th wedding anniversary today. Back when we got married we went to the Paramount Theater, and after the show we came down to your restaurant. We told you we just got married, and you set us up with a bowl of chili for our wedding dinner. When we left here, you gave us a menu as a souvenir. So we thought we would come back on our fiftieth wedding anniversary, have a bowl of chili, and see if you'd like to have that old menu back." We had never kept those old menus, so we were pretty happy to get one. We keep that menu on the wall, and we put a copy of it in this book.

Eva and I hope you enjoy this book as much as we've enjoyed putting it together. When you're in Nashville, stop in for a sample of our chili. We'd love to see you. And we'd love it if you'd bring us a special thought. May the warm grace of God's pure love bless your life as He has Eva's and mine. God be with you always.

Frank Varallo

Frank Varallo, Sr. with his family. Frank, Jr. is dressed in white, seated
on his mother's knee

Thoughts from the Bottom of a Chili Bowl

Horse Sense
& Chestnuts

All that is necessary for triumph of evil is for good people to do nothing.

❧

There is no right way to do something that is wrong.

❧

A skeptic is one who won't take know for an answer.

❧

Do not test the depth of the river with both feet.

Horse Sense & Chestnuts

*T*he more you know, the more you know you don't know.

~

*N*othing will increase your golf score like witnesses.

~

*W*henever things sound simple, it turns out there is one thing you didn't hear.

~

*T*he only difference between a weed and a flower is a judgment.

Thoughts from the Bottom of a Chili Bowl

Don't kick a pulling mule.

Horse Sense & Chestnuts

$\mathcal{T}$he eighth wonder of the world is the person who can remember the other seven.

⌁

$\mathcal{W}$ith all its wonders, science has found no cure for stupidity.

⌁

$\mathcal{O}$ne trouble with trouble is that it usually starts out like fun.

⌁

$\mathcal{A}$n error is like a leak in the roof of your house—the damage it can do depends on how long it takes you to fix it.

Thoughts from the Bottom of a Chili Bowl

*E*ven if you are a minority of one, the truth is still the truth.

~

*T*here is nothing like a little experience to upset a theory.

~

*U*topia is the good ol' days plus all the modern conveniences.

~

*D*on't worry about it; it ain't going to be all right anyway.

Horse Sense & Chestnuts

*L*aziness is just getting your rest before you get tired.

~

*T*he water that supports the boat can also sink it.

~

*T*he right to do something does not make doing it right.

~

*B*eware of the high cost of low living.

Thoughts from the Bottom of a Chili Bowl

$\mathcal{T}$he things you can't forget are the things you don't want to remember.

~

$\mathcal{E}$verything said has been said before, the trouble is remembering it.

~

$\mathcal{I}$f Noah had been truly wise he would have swatted those two mosquitos.

~

$\mathcal{I}$f you think education is expensive, try ignorance.

Horse Sense & Chestnuts

$\mathcal{I}$t takes courage to stand up and speak. It also takes courage to sit down and listen.

~

$\mathcal{I}$f you have half a mind to do something, it would be wise to check with the other half before doing it.

~

$\mathcal{E}$ven the wool you are trying to pull over my eyes is half cotton.

~

$\mathcal{I}$t takes both rain and sunshine to make a rainbow.

Thoughts from the Bottom of a Chili Bowl

10

***Stop believing
in Santa Claus
and you get
underwear.***

Horse Sense & Chestnuts

*L*ife is what happens to you while you are making other plans.

~

A person's mind stretched by a new idea never goes back to its original dimensions.

~

*H*ate is a prolonged manner of suicide.

~

*W*e crucify ourselves between two thieves: regret for yesterday and fear for tomorrow.

Thoughts from the Bottom of a Chili Bowl

$\mathscr{I}$t is not so important where we come from as it is where we are going.

～

$\mathscr{E}$xperience is a hard teacher; she tests first and teaches afterward.

～

$\mathscr{A}$ssociate with people of good quality if you esteem your own reputation; it is better to be alone than in bad company.

～

$\mathscr{A}$ wise person learns to enjoy things without owning them.

Horse Sense & Chestnuts

13

*A*n intellectual is a person who takes more words than necessary to tell more than they know.

~

*M*ost of the mountains we have to climb we build ourselves.

~

*D*on't try to drown your sorrows—they know how to swim.

~

*C*ourage is fear that has said its prayers.

Thoughts from the Bottom of a Chili Bowl

*Beware of a
narrow mind
with a wide
mouth.*

Horse Sense & Chestnuts

15

*E*xperience is the best teacher if you can afford the lessons.

~

*T*hey who lie down with dogs shall rise up with fleas.

~

*T*here's always free cheese in the mousetrap.

~

*R*oad maps tell motorists everything they want to know except how to fold them up again.

Thoughts from the Bottom of a Chili Bowl

$\mathcal{I}$t is better to have loafed and lost than
never to have loafed at all.

~

$\mathcal{T}$he real problem with leisure time is how to
keep others from using yours.

~

$\mathcal{T}$he way you spend Christmas is more
important than how much you spend.

~

$\mathcal{T}$hat which you cannot give away you do not
possess. It possesses you.

Horse Sense & Chestnuts

*S*tatistics are no substitute for judgment.

~

*E*xperience is a wonderful thing; it enables you to recognize a mistake when you make it again.

~

*I*t is not best that we should all think alike. It is differences of opinion that make horse races.

~

*I*f the only tool you have is a hammer, you tend to see every problem as a nail.

Thoughts from the Bottom of a Chili Bowl

*T*here is no lawyer who can draw up an agreement that is better than a handshake of an honest person.

❧

*T*he wise learn more from fools than fools learn from the wise.

❧

*T*he chains of habit are too weak to be felt, but they are too strong to be broken.

❧

*T*he unfortunate thing about this world is that good habits are so much easier to give up than bad ones.

Horse Sense & Chestnuts

*T*hree rules for healthy teeth: brush after every meal, see your dentist often, and mind your own business.

❧

A good example has twice the value of good advice.

❧

A good memory is fine but the ability to forget is better.

❧

*W*orry is interest paid on trouble before it is due.

Thoughts from the Bottom of a Chili Bowl

Even a mole may instruct a philosopher in the art of digging.

Horse Sense & Chestnuts

You can lead a horse to water but you can't make him drink. But you can put salt on his food to make him thirsty.

~

Only the second rate are safe from the jealousy of others.

~

Where there is love in the heart, there is room in the home.

~

How much we admire the wisdom of those who come to us for advice.

Thoughts from the Bottom of a Chili Bowl

*I*f you wonder what the world is coming to,
remember so did your grandfather.

❧

*A*dvice is like snow: the softer it falls the
deeper it goes.

❧

A bird never flies so far that its tail doesn't
follow.

❧

*L*ife doesn't give any make-up tests.

Horse Sense & Chestnuts

A fault recognized is half corrected.

~

*N*ever mistake knowledge for wisdom—one helps you make a living, the other helps you make a life.

~

*T*he man who trims himself to suit everybody will soon whittle himself away.

~

*O*ne thing that proves there is intelligent life in the universe is that they steer clear of us.

Thoughts from the Bottom of a Chili Bowl

*E*verybody knows somebody, and that
somebody might know you.

~

*E*ducation is what you get when reading the
small print.

~

*E*xperience is not what happens to you, it's
what you do with what happens to you.

~

*T*he reason some people get lost in thought is
because it is unfamiliar territory.

Horse Sense & Chestnuts

$\mathcal{H}$ow long we live is limited, but how much we learn is not.

~

$\mathcal{T}$he easiest person to deceive is yourself.

~

$\mathcal{C}$ommon sense is not so common.

~

$\mathcal{E}$xperience is what you get when you don't.

Thoughts from the Bottom of a Chili Bowl

Young Frank Varallo, Jr.

Frank Varallo at the steam table, serving up Varallo's famous chili

Thoughts from the Bottom of a Chili Bowl

Do's & Don't's

*I*f you don't practice what you preach, what you preach won't be practiced.

❧

*S*ome people pay a compliment like they dug into their pocket for it.

❧

*T*hose who spend today boasting about the wonderful things they will do tomorrow probably spent yesterday doing the same thing.

❧

*P*oliteness is a small price to pay for the affection of others.

Do's & Don't's

A rumor is as hard to unspread as butter.

Thoughts from the Bottom of a Chili Bowl

*I*f you fly off the handle, you usually make a bad landing.

❧

*T*act is the art of not saying everything you think.

❧

*A*lways taste your words before you let them pass your teeth.

❧

*P*atience is a bitter plant but it has a sweet fruit.

Do's & Don't's

*T*he more you talk, the less people remember
what you say.

~

A person's own good manners are the best
security against the rudeness of others.

~

*Y*ou can tell more about people by what they
say about others than you can by what others
say about them.

~

*T*here is an element of truth in every idea that
lasts long enough to be called corny.

Thoughts from the Bottom of a Chili Bowl

*I*f you are patient in one moment of ang/
you will escape a hundred days of sorrow.

~

*M*ost people who sing their own praises can't
carry a tune.

~

*M*any things are opened by mistake but none
so often as the mouth.

~

*A*lways remember to stop talking before
people stop listening.

Do's & Don't's

*T*emper is what gets most of us in trouble.
Pride is what keeps us there.

~

A slip of the foot you may soon get over, but
a slip of the tongue you may never recover.

~

*T*act is the ability to make someone feel at
home when you wish they were.

~

*I*t is hard to believe that people are telling the
truth when you know you would lie if you
were in their place.

Thoughts from the Bottom of a Chili Bowl

*B*e sincere with your compliments. Most people can tell the difference between sugar and saccharine.

❧

*B*e sure you have your brain in gear before you put your mouth in motion.

❧

*E*xpress a mean opinion of yourself occasionally; it will show your friends that you know how to tell the truth.

❧

*E*ven a fish wouldn't get caught if it just kept its mouth shut.

Do's & Don't's

Every time you talk your mind is on parade.

Thoughts from the Bottom of a Chili Bowl

*M*odesty is the act of drawing attention to
whatever it is you are being humble about.

~

*I*f you can't write it and sign it, don't say it.

~

*I*t takes an honest man to tell if he is tired or
just lazy.

~

*T*act is the art of making a point without
making an enemy.

Do's & Don't's

$\mathscr{G}$ossip, unlike river water, flows both ways.

~

$\mathscr{B}$y the time someone says, "To make a long
story short," it's too late.

~

$\mathscr{T}$he most difficult secret for people to keep is
the opinion they have of themselves.

~

$\mathscr{A}$ bore is somebody who goes on talking
while you are trying to interrupt.

Thoughts from the Bottom of a Chili Bowl

Frank's brother, Nick Varallo, with daughter Aurelia

$\mathcal{R}$umors without a leg to stand on still have a way of getting around.

~

$\mathcal{T}$he chances are if you're trying to make an impression, that's the impression you'll make.

~

$\mathcal{T}$he truth is not always dressed up for the evening.

~

$\mathcal{O}$ne way to prevent a conversation from being boring is to say the wrong thing.

Thoughts from the Bottom of a Chili Bowl

$\mathscr{D}$on't advertise your troubles, there's no market for them.

❧

$\mathscr{P}$eople who talk too much for their own good don't do much for the listeners either.

❧

$\mathscr{A}$ fool can ask more questions than a wise man can answer.

❧

$\mathscr{A}$ sharp tongue is no indication of a keen mind.

Do's & Don't's

*A*lways tell the truth and you won't have to
remember what you said.

~

*W*ith a sweet tongue and kindness you can
drag an elephant by a hair.

~

*H*onesty is the best policy, because it has little
competition.

~

*J*ust because you find fault doesn't mean you
have to report it.

Thoughts from the Bottom of a Chili Bowl

$\mathcal{N}$othing turns fact into fiction faster than
word of mouth.

~

$\mathcal{T}$he reason we make a long story short is so
we can tell another.

~

$\mathcal{H}$ow you say it can be just as important as
what you say.

~

$\mathcal{N}$one are so fond of secrets as those that do
not mean to keep them.

Do's & Don't's

A closed mouth gathers no foot.

Thoughts from the Bottom of a Chili Bowl

*W*hen someone says "I hope you don't mind if I tell you this," chances are you will.

~

A gossip is one who can give you all the details without knowing any of the facts.

~

A lady is a woman who makes a man act like a gentleman.

~

A secret is a secret only when one person knows it.

Do's & Don't's

$\mathscr{A}$ single fact will often spoil an interesting argument.

❧

$\mathscr{C}$onscience is that still small voice that is sometimes too loud for comfort.

❧

$\mathscr{H}$alf truths tell less than half the story.

❧

$\mathscr{S}$wallow your pride occasionally. It is calorie free and won't give you indigestion.

Thoughts from the Bottom of a Chili Bowl

*M*ost of us can forgive and forget; we just don't want the other person to forget what we forgave.

~

*T*o handle yourself use your head; to handle others use your heart.

~

*W*e grow a little every time we do not take advantage of somebody's weakness.

~

*T*he way some people find fault, you'd think there was a reward.

Do's & Don't's

*D*ishonesty is like a boomerang—about the time you think all is well, it hits you in the back of the head.

❧

*A*n eye for an eye only ends up making the whole world blind.

❧

*A*dvice is like cooking—you should try it before you feed it to others.

❧

*N*othing will make your sense of humor disappear faster than someone asking where it is.

Thoughts from the Bottom of a Chili Bowl

$\mathcal{T}$he fragrance always stays in the hand that gives the rose.

$\sim$

$\mathcal{N}$ever be haughty to the humble; never be humble to the haughty.

$\sim$

$\mathcal{N}$othing is as hard to do gracefully as getting down off your high horse.

$\sim$

$\mathcal{I}$f you look for the best in people, it will keep you so busy you won't have time to notice the worst.

Do's & Don't's

51

$\mathcal{D}$on't carry a grudge; while you are carrying
it the other person is out dancing.

~

$\mathcal{F}$or your heart's sake, don't run up stairs and
run down people.

~

$\mathcal{H}$ow you win shows some of your character;
how you lose shows all of it.

~

$\mathcal{T}$he person who takes but never gives
may last for years but never lives.

Thoughts from the Bottom of a Chili Bowl

Blessed are they who have nothing to say and cannot be persuaded to say it.

Do's & Don't's

53

*I*f you have more than you need, give to
those who need more than they have.

~

*T*hose people prove their worth who can
make us want to listen when they are with us
and think when they are gone.

~

*P*atience is a virtue that carries a lot of wait.

~

*P*rejudice is weighing the facts with your
thumb on the scale.

Thoughts from the Bottom of a Chili Bowl

The greatest gift we can give to others is a good example.

~

The only people you should want to get even with are those who have helped you.

~

One person practicing sportsmanship is far better than fifty preaching it.

~

The best way to knock the chip off a person's shoulder is to pat them on the back.

Do's & Don't's

$\mathcal{T}$he world doesn't need go-getters as much as it needs go-givers.

❧

$\mathcal{W}$hen you stop giving you stop living.

❧

$\mathcal{W}$ho takes revenge in less than twenty years acts in haste.

❧

$\mathcal{W}$rite injuries in dust, benefits in marble.

Thoughts from the Bottom of a Chili Bowl

$\mathcal{Y}$ou can judge the character of a person by how they treat people who can do nothing for them.

~

$\mathcal{W}$hen you are good when nobody is looking, that's integrity.

~

$\mathcal{C}$onceit is that disease that makes everyone sick except the one who has it.

Do's & Don't's

Actors and actresses often enjoyed dinner at Varallo's after their performances
at the Paramount theatre

Thoughts from the Bottom of a Chili Bowl

Workin' &
Winnin'

*T*here never has been a statue erected in the honor of someone who left well enough alone.

~

*T*he more ploughing and weeding, the better the crop.

~

*T*ake time to sharpen the saw and the wood will be easier to cut.

~

*P*eople won't remember how fast you did the job. They will only remember how well you did it.

Workin' & Winnin'

Frank and Eva on their wedding day in 1937

$\mathscr{A}$ good manager makes work easier—not harder—for people to do their job.

~

$\mathscr{M}$ost people like their jobs. It's the work they can't stand.

~

$\mathscr{M}$ake what you do today important; after all, you are exchanging a day of your life for it.

~

$\mathscr{D}$on't itch for anything you are not willing to scratch for.

Workin' & Winnin'

$\mathcal{T}$he wish bone will never replace the back bone.

~

$\mathcal{H}$ard work is the yeast that raises the dough.

~

$\mathcal{P}$eople willing to roll up their sleeves seldom lose their shirt.

~

$\mathcal{A}$n ounce of accomplishment is worth a ton of good intentions.

Thoughts from the Bottom of a Chili Bowl

$\mathcal{A}$nybody who isn't pulling his weight is
probably pushing his luck.

❧

$\mathcal{S}$ome people are like blisters—they don't
show up until all the work is done.

❧

$\mathcal{T}$he more help you have in your garden, the
less it will belong to you.

❧

$\mathcal{A}$ll the flowers of tomorrow are in the seeds
of today.

Workin' & Winnin'

A camel is a horse that was put together by a committee.

Thoughts from the Bottom of a Chili Bowl

$\mathscr{A}$ good boss is one who takes a little more of the blame and a little less of the credit.

~

$\mathscr{W}$ell done is better than well said.

~

$\mathscr{T}$hose who never do more than they are paid for will never be paid for more than they do.

~

$\mathscr{W}$hen your work speaks for itself, don't interrupt.

Workin' & Winnin'

67

*I*t isn't so much how busy you are but why you are busy. A bee is praised and a mosquito is swatted.

❧

*T*he brain is a wonderful organ. It starts working the moment you get up in the morning and doesn't stop until you get to the office.

❧

*T*he reason worry kills more people than work is that there are more people who worry than work.

❧

*L*ive today as if it were your last, but work as if you would live forever.

Thoughts from the Bottom of a Chili Bowl

$\mathcal{T}$he work of the world does not wait to be done by perfect people.

~

$\mathcal{K}$nowledge is power only when it's turned on.

~

$\mathcal{T}$he path of least resistance is always downhill.

~

$\mathcal{T}$he only thing wrong with doing nothing is that you never know when you are finished.

Workin' & Winnin'

*N*othing wilts faster than laurels that are rested upon.

~

*L*aziness travels so slowly that poverty soon overtakes it.

~

*D*on't waste time looking for short cuts to anyplace worth going.

~

*T*alent is like a picture taken by a camera. To amount to anything, it needs developing.

Thoughts from the Bottom of a Chili Bowl

$\mathcal{P}$eople who are resting on their laurels are wearing them on the wrong end.

~

$\mathcal{D}$on't wait until your lights go out before you buy candles.

~

$\mathcal{D}$o not squander time; it is the stuff that life is made of.

~

$\mathcal{D}$ig a well before you get thirsty.

Workin' & Winnin'

*I*f it weren't for the last minute, a lot of things wouldn't get done.

❧

*T*he computer's a great invention. There are just as many mistakes as ever, but they are nobody's fault.

❧

*A*ll things come to those who wait, but sometimes it's just the leftovers from the ones who got there first.

Thoughts from the Bottom of a Chili Bowl

Even a blind hog will find an acorn every once in a while.

Workin' & Winnin'

A tool unto itself is of little importance, but put in the proper hands it can create a masterpiece.

~

To think too long about doing a thing often becomes its undoing.

~

*S*elf-discipline is when your conscience tells you to do something and you don't talk back.

~

A mistake at least proves somebody stopped talking long enough to do something.

Thoughts from the Bottom of a Chili Bowl

*E*verything comes to those who hustle while
they wait.

~

*T*he road to success is always under
construction.

~

*H*e who does not hope to win has
already lost.

~

*I*f at first you do succeed, try to hide your
astonishment.

Workin' & Winnin'

What kills a skunk is the publicity it gives itself.

Thoughts from the Bottom of a Chili Bowl

*N*o formula for success will work if you don't.

~

*O*ne measure of success is doing what you like
to do and making a living at it.

~

*T*here may not be a formula for success, but
there is one for failure: try to please everybody.

~

*Y*ou can have anything in the world you
want simply by helping enough other people
get what they want.

Workin' & Winnin'

*W*inners make a commitment while losers
only make a promise.

~

*F*ailure isn't fatal and success isn't final.

~

*N*ever insult an alligator until after you have
crossed the river.

~

*T*o win is not always success and to lose is
not always failure.

Thoughts from the Bottom of a Chili Bowl

$\mathscr{T}$he unfortunate thing about being a success is
finding people who are happy for you.

~

$\mathscr{T}$here is no great pleasure in achieving success
if nothing ever stood in the way of it.

~

$\mathscr{I}$t's not too late to be what you might have
been.

~

$\mathscr{I}$f you can't do great things, do small things
in a great way.

Workin' & Winnin'

Success is simply failure turned inside out.

Thoughts from the Bottom of a Chili Bowl

*Y*ou can't build a reputation on what you are going to do.

❧

*I*f you want your dreams to come true, don't oversleep.

❧

*I*n the game of life, it's easier to see the goalposts if you keep your chin up.

❧

*L*ooking ahead keeps one from falling behind.

Workin' & Winnin'

All the people who work hard don't succeed,
but the ones who do succeed work hard.

~

The winds and waves are always on the side
of the ablest navigators.

~

You only have to be 10% better at what you
do than most people to go 100% farther.

~

We make our choices, then our choices make
us.

Thoughts from the Bottom of a Chili Bowl

Almost killed a
duck don't make
soup.

Workin' & Winnin'

$\mathcal{W}$e travel this road but once, but if we play our cards right, once is enough.

❧

$\mathcal{S}$trength does not come from physical capacity; it comes from an indomitable will.

❧

$\mathcal{T}$he trouble with being a leader today is that you can't be sure if people are following you or chasing you.

❧

$\mathcal{T}$hings turn out the best for those who make the best of the way things turn out.

Thoughts from the Bottom of a Chili Bowl

*I*f you can't see the bright side, polish the
dull side.

❧

A good life requires some learning, some
earning, and some yearning.

❧

A person may stumble and fall many times in
life, but they are not a failure until they say,
"Who pushed me?"

❧

*Y*ou are what you think you are, and you
will become what you think you are sooner
or later.

Workin' & Winnin'

One of the hardest things in life to learn is which bridge to cross and which to burn.

❧

What's right is not always popular, and what's popular is not always right.

❧

You will always pay for a short cut in the long run.

❧

If you want to be seen, stand up. If you want to be heard, speak up. If you want to be appreciated, sit down.

Thoughts from the Bottom of a Chili Bowl

*I*t's not what you are that holds you back,
but what you think you are not.

~

*L*earn from other people's mistakes. You
won't live long enough to make them all
yourself.

~

A person cannot discover new oceans unless
he has courage to lose sight of the shore.

~

*B*e content with what you have but not with
what you are.

Workin' & Winnin'

Change favors the prepared mind.

Thoughts from the Bottom of a Chili Bowl

$\mathcal{C}$ontentment comes not from riches but from simple wants.

~

$\mathcal{D}$on't count the passing days; make the passing days count.

~

$\mathcal{D}$ifficulties are supposed to make us better, not bitter.

~

$\mathcal{D}$o what's right—this will gratify some and astonish others.

Workin' & Winnin'

*I*f you want to break a bad habit, drop it.

❧

*I*f life is a grind, use it to sharpen your character.

❧

*I*t is better to know less than to know a lot that isn't so.

❧

*I*t isn't the load that weighs us down; it's the way we carry it.

Thoughts from the Bottom of a Chili Bowl

*A*lways put off till tomorrow what you shouldn't do at all.

❧

*O*pportunity never comes. It's here.

❧

*P*eople that worry the most have the most time to worry.

❧

*S*ome grow under responsibilities. Others merely swell.

Workin' & Winnin'

Solving problems is easy; it's living with the
solutions that is tough.

~

Time is money; spend it wisely.

~

The world steps aside for those who know
where they are going.

~

Think how smart most of us would be if
we retained as much of what we read as
what we eat.

Thoughts from the Bottom of a Chili Bowl

Pray for a good harvest, but continue to hoe.

Workin' & Winnin'

*T*here are no degrees of honesty.

~

*T*here is something positive in most negative things.

~

*U*ntil you make peace with who you are, you'll never be content with what you have.

~

*P*rogress begins with the belief that what is necessary is possible.

Thoughts from the Bottom of a Chili Bowl

*T*here is only one thing worse than hardness of heart and that is softness of head.

~

*O*ne part of knowledge consists of being ignorant about those things that are not worth knowing.

~

*P*eople show what they are by what they do with what they have.

~

*A*n opportunity grasped and used produces at least one other opportunity.

Workin' & Winnin'

A good angle to approach any problem is the try-angle.

~

*B*eaten paths are for beaten people.

~

*W*hat you think of people is what they think of you.

Thoughts from the Bottom of a Chili Bowl

*W*hat you see is what you look for.

~

*W*hatever your lot in life, build something on
it.

~

*W*hatever you decide to do, you can find
someone who will be against it.

~

*W*henever you can, hang around the lucky.

Workin' & Winnin'

*I*f your life takes a turn for the worse,
remember that you are the one who is driving.

~

*L*ife is like a grindstone, and whether it grinds
you down or polishes you depends on the stuff
you are made of.

~

*T*he ones that have all the luck are the ones
that don't depend on it.

~

*I*f you take too long in deciding what to do
with your life, you'll find that you've done it.

Thoughts from the Bottom of a Chili Bowl

*Life is like a
poker game—
trust everybody
but cut the cards.*

Workin' & Winnin

$\mathscr{M}$any important things are done by folks too dumb to know they can't be done.

❧

$\mathscr{W}$hy not go out on a limb, isn't that where the fruit is?

❧

$\mathscr{C}$hoice—not chance—determines one's destiny.

❧

$\mathscr{Y}$ou can change the mind of a person who possesses an idea, but never one who is possessed by one.

Thoughts from the Bottom of a Chili Bowl

They that tooteth not their own horn, the same shall not be tooted.

Workin' & Winnin'

Parade in old downtown Nashville

Thoughts from the Bottom of a Chili Bowl

Courtin'
& Kin

Often a good marriage depends on leaving a
few things a day left unsaid.

~

It is human nature to do something that is a
pleasure, which is why the human race
continues to double every forty years.

~

The great secret of a successful marriage is to
treat all disasters as incidents and none of the
incidents as disasters.

~

Happiness is knowing that you married your
best friend.

Courtin' & Kin

Frank Varallo with a local business owner (note the juke box on the wall)

*T*here are two important expressions that will keep your marriage bright: "I love you" and "Maybe you're right."

~

*I*t's amazing how many marriages are on a 50-50 basis—he blames her and she blames him.

~

*I*n a courtship the heart beats so loudly it blocks out the sound of the mind.

~

A successful marriage requires falling in love many times but always with the same person.

Courtin' & Kin

A man always feels better after a few winks, especially if she winks back.

~

*B*eauty is not discovered with the eye but with the soul.

~

*O*h, to be only half as wonderful as my child thought I was, but only half as stupid as my teenager thinks I am.

~

*H*e who brags about his family tree has first done a good trimming job.

Thoughts from the Bottom of a Chili Bowl

*A*utomation is the technical process that does all the work while you just sit there. When you were younger, it was called mother.

❧

*D*on't confuse your children by mixing good counsel with bad conduct.

❧

*I*f you can't do anything with your kids, it's probably because you don't.

❧

*T*he surest way to make it hard for your children is to make it soft for them.

Courtin' & Kin

*I*f you want your children to keep their feet on the ground, put some responsibility on their shoulders.

~

*W*here the parents do too much for their children, the children will not do much for themselves.

~

*W*e never know the love of our parents for us until we become parents.

~

*T*oo often we give children answers to remember rather than problems to solve.

Thoughts from the Bottom of a Chili Bowl

110

No matter how old
a mother is she
watches her
middle-aged
children for signs
of improvement.

Courtin' & Kin

A child is born with a need for love and
never outgrows it.

~

A child, like your stomach, doesn't need all
you can afford to give it.

~

A broken home is the world's greatest wreck.

~

*T*he man who claims that he never made a
mistake in his life generally has a wife who did.

Thoughts from the Bottom of a Chili Bowl

Varallo's customer with the policeman
who watched over the restaurant for many years

Local high school teams, such as this 1941 football team, often "hung out" at Varallo's

Thoughts from the Bottom of a Chili Bowl

Friends
& Grins

A friend is someone who goes around saying nice things about you behind your back.

~

*Y*ou can't sow jealousy and hate and reap love and friendship.

~

*M*ay we have more and more friends and need them less and less.

~

*T*he best way to wipe out a friendship is to sponge on it.

Friends & Grins

*A*lways forgive your enemies;
nothing annoys them so much.

~

*F*orget what you do for others, but don't
forget what they do for you.

~

*T*o have fewer enemies, make friends of them.

~

*T*he oil of courtesy will reduce a lot of
friction.

Thoughts from the Bottom of a Chili Bowl

$\mathcal{C}$onsideration for others can mean taking a
wing instead of a drumstick.

~

$\mathcal{W}$hen we get too busy to think of others, we
are too busy.

~

$\mathcal{I}$f you want an accounting of your worth,
count your friends.

~

$\mathcal{A}$ friend is one who walks in when all others
walk out.

Friends & Grins

The best antiques are old friends.

Thoughts from the Bottom of a Chili Bowl

$\mathcal{F}$riends are made by many acts, but lost by
only one.

❧

$\mathcal{H}$ating people is like burning down your own
house to get rid of a rat.

❧

$\mathcal{G}$etting other people to like you is only the
other side of liking them.

❧

$\mathcal{T}$he smallest deed is more meaningful than the
greatest intention.

Friends & Grins

1948–49 Varallo's Girls' Bowling Team

$\mathcal{L}$ove sees through a telescope—not a microscope.

～

$\mathcal{A}$ Christmas gift that is almost certain to be returned is love.

～

$\mathcal{E}$verybody has to be somebody to somebody to be anybody.

～

$\mathcal{T}$he best gifts are tied with heartstrings.

Friends & Grins

$\mathcal{D}$on't bore your friends with your troubles;
tell them to your enemies, they will enjoy
hearing them.

~

$\mathcal{A}$ hug is the perfect gift—one size fits all and
nobody minds if you exchange it.

~

$\mathcal{T}$hey who can't forgive burn the bridge over
which they too must pass.

~

$\mathcal{T}$he more a person knows, the more they
forgive.

Thoughts from the Bottom of a Chili Bowl

*T*he secret of happiness is to count your blessings while others are adding up their troubles.

~

*T*o be truly happy you must have three things: something to do, someone to love, and something to hope for.

~

*M*ost smiles are started by other smiles.

~

A smile is a curve that very often can set a lot of things straight.

Friends & Grins

Happiness sneaks in through a door you didn't know you left open.

Thoughts from the Bottom of a Chili Bowl

A smile can add a great deal to one's face value.

⁓

*M*ake one person happy each day—even if it's yourself.

⁓

*W*hen there is love in your heart it will show on your face.

⁓

*H*appiness is like jam—it's hard to spread even a little without getting some on yourself.

Friends & Grins

*H*appy are the people who can laugh at themselves. They will never cease to be amused.

❧

A smile is an inexpensive way to improve your looks.

❧

*H*appiness makes everyone beautiful.

❧

*N*ever miss an opportunity to make others happy, even if you have to leave them alone to do it.

Thoughts from the Bottom of a Chili Bowl

$\mathcal{A}$ smile is a wrinkle that should not be
removed.

❧

$\mathcal{H}$appiness is not our destination, but our
mode of transportation.

❧

$\mathcal{L}$aughter is the universal language; it means
joy and gladness, and needs no further
interpretation.

❧

$\mathcal{L}$ife is a mirror; if you frown at it, it will
frown back; if you smile, it returns the greeting.

Friends & Grins

A major cause of unhappiness is overestimating the happiness of others.

❧

A smile is the shortest distance between two people.

❧

*I*t's all right to take a trip to nostalgia now and then as long as you don't set up housekeeping.

❧

I would rather sit on a pumpkin and have it all to myself than to be crowded on a velvet cushion.

Thoughts from the Bottom of a Chili Bowl

$\mathcal{T}$he invariable mark of wisdom is to see the miraculous in the common.

❧

$\mathcal{F}$or every problem there is a solution, even if it is learning to live with the problem.

❧

$\mathcal{A}$ pessimist is one who complains about the noise when opportunity knocks.

❧

$\mathcal{A}$n optimist sees a light that isn't there. A pessimist comes along and blows it out.

Friends & Grins

A smile is the cheapest facelift you can get.

Thoughts from the Bottom of a Chili Bowl

$\mathcal{T}$he things you do when you don't have to do them determine what you will be when you no longer can help it.

~

$\mathcal{W}$e tire of those pleasures we take, but never those that we give.

~

$\mathcal{W}$hy is it so hard to forget the things we would like to forget and so easy to forget the things we would like to remember?

~

$\mathcal{E}$njoy your own life without comparing it with that of another.

Friends & Grins

What cannot bend
may break.

Thoughts from the Bottom of a Chili Bowl

Girls enjoying Varallo's chili, or Varallo's waiters?

The Varallo's (from left) Geny (originator of the "thoughts for the day"), Jimmy, Vici, Franky, Eva, and Frank

Thoughts from the Bottom of a Chili Bowl

Politics & Pocketbooks

$\mathcal{V}$ote for the man who promises the least and you will be least disappointed.

~

$\mathcal{I}$t's every American's duty to support the government, but not necessarily in the style to which it has become accustomed.

~

$\mathcal{N}$othing makes it harder for a politician to remember campaign promises than getting elected.

~

$\mathcal{A}$ lame duck is a politician whose goose has been cooked.

Politics & Pocketbooks

$\mathcal{M}$any politicians are great contortionists; they can straddle a fence and have an ear to the ground at the same time.

~

$\mathcal{M}$ost people would like to tend to their own business if the government would only give it back.

~

$\mathcal{A}$nything that keeps a politician humble is healthy for democracy.

~

$\mathcal{O}$ther employees would do no better than congressmen if the boss showed an interest in them only once in two years.

Thoughts from the Bottom of a Chili Bowl

A politician is someone who can make waves and then convince you he is the only one who can save the ship.

~

*P*overty is catching—you get it from politicians.

~

*T*he sum total of our national debt is some total.

~

*T*he integrity of a nation is best judged by how it takes care of its elderly, its handicapped, its sick, and its children.

Politics & Pocketbooks

$\mathcal{F}$reedom is like the air we breathe. We can't see it or smell it or hear it. But if we lost it we'd suffocate.

❧

$\mathcal{I}$t is difficult to tell young people that they should have respect for authority when we pay a third baseman three times what we pay the President of the United States.

❧

$\mathcal{Y}$ou can tell when people are well informed—their views are pretty much like your own.

❧

$\mathcal{M}$oney is a good servant but a poor master.

Thoughts from the Bottom of a Chili Bowl

$\mathcal{N}$o matter how often it is shown that money doesn't buy happiness, we are always willing to give it another chance.

~

$\mathcal{T}$he only two who can live as cheaply as one are a horse and a fly.

~

$\mathcal{T}$wo can live as cheaply as one, but who wants to live that cheap?

~

$\mathcal{M}$ost people don't spend more than they earn—they just spend it quicker than they earn it.

Politics & Pocketbooks

Death and taxes
may always be
with us, but at
least death
doesn't get any
worse.

Thoughts from the Bottom of a Chili Bowl

*H*ow empty the life that is filled only with
things.

~

*I*t is not in riches that we find contentment
but in contentment that we discover riches.

~

*T*he rich may not live longer, but it sure seems
like it to their poor relatives.

~

*T*he income tax has made more liars out of
people than golf has.

Politics & Pocketbooks

$\mathcal{M}$oney does not make you happy, but it does quiet the nerves.

❧

$\mathcal{T}$here was a time when a fool and his money were soon parted. Now it happens to everybody.

❧

$\mathcal{P}$eople call it take-home pay because there is no other place you can afford to go with it.

❧

$\mathcal{T}$he idea is to make a little money first, then make a little money last.

Thoughts from the Bottom of a Chili Bowl

*T*he man who loves money will never be
satisfied with money.

❧

*T*he trouble with saving for a rainy day is
that most folks don't start until it begins to
cloud up.

❧

*M*oney can't buy everything, but it certainly
puts you in a great bargaining position.

❧

*B*y the time you finish paying for a house in
the country, it's no longer in the country.

Politics & Pocketbooks

A fool and his money are soon parted, but how did he get it in the first place?

❧

*W*e're better at deciding what we would do with a million dollars than what we're going to do without it.

❧

*N*othing seems to bring on an emergency as quickly as putting money aside in case of one.

❧

*P*utting something away for a rainy day requires a whole lot longer stretch of dry weather than it used to.

Thoughts from the Bottom of a Chili Bowl

*Next to being shot
at and missed,
there is nothing
quite as
satisfying as
getting an income
tax refund.*

Politics & Pocketbooks

When a leisure time activity begins to cost money, it's called a hobby.

᷍

It is what we value, not what we have, that makes us rich.

᷍

Car sickness is the feeling you get every month when the payment comes due.

᷍

There is something magic about Christmas time. It's when your money does a disappearing act.

Thoughts from the Bottom of a Chili Bowl

$\mathcal{H}$ealth insurance is like wearing a hospital gown; you only think you are fully covered.

~

$\mathcal{A}$ great actor can bring tears to your eyes, but so can an auto mechanic.

~

$\mathcal{J}$ust be glad you are not getting all the government you are paying for.

Politics & Pocketbooks

Pat Patterson, an employee who has served Varallo's for over fifty
years. Note the sign above him.

Thoughts from the Bottom of a Chili Bowl

Gettin' Old
& Gettin'
Good

*Y*ou are middle-aged when doubts take the
place of your dreams.

❧

*A*n old timer is a person who remembers the
days when people stopped spending when they
ran out of money.

❧

A good thing about getting old is that all
those things you always wanted and couldn't
afford, you no longer want.

❧

*M*iddle age is when we can do just as much
as we ever could, but would rather not.

Gettin' Old & Gettin' Good

Pat Boone, a Varallo's regular, and his parents with Mrs. Eva and Mr. Frank

Middle age starts the day you become more interested in how long your car will last than in how fast it will go.

Gettin' Old & Gettin' Good

*T*o truly appreciate the beauty and dignity of an old face, you have to read between the lines.

❧

*T*he older you get, the smarter your parents and grandparents get.

❧

*I*f youth but knew and old age but could.

❧

*P*eople are as young as their dreams and as old as their doubts.

Thoughts from the Bottom of a Chili Bowl

*C*ount your age by your friends not years;
count your life by smiles not tears.

~

*O*ne good thing about middle-age spread—it
brings people closer together.

~

*T*he metallic years are when you've got silver
in your hair, gold in your teeth, and lead in
your bottom.

~

*Y*ou can't turn back the clock, but you can
wind it up again.

Gettin' Old & Gettin' Good

$\mathcal{Y}$ou know you're getting old when. . .

You bend down to tie your shoes and wonder
what else you can do while you are down
there.

Your little black book contains only names
ending in M.D.

You know all the answers, but nobody is
asking you questions.

You get out of the shower and you are glad the
mirror is all fogged up.

Thoughts from the Bottom of a Chili Bowl

$\mathcal{A}$s people grow older and wiser, they talk less and say more.

~

$\mathcal{Y}$ou are getting old if it takes you longer to rest than it did to get tired.

~

$\mathcal{A}$ge alone does not bring wisdom.

~

$\mathcal{S}$ometimes it's better not to know now what you didn't know then.

Gettin' Old & Gettin' Good

Time may be a great healer, but it is a lousy beautician.

Thoughts from the Bottom of a Chili Bowl

$\mathcal{N}$ever trust people who have to change their tone when talking to God.

~

$\mathcal{Y}$our religion is what you do when the sermon is over.

~

$\mathcal{G}$od can do great things through the person who doesn't care who gets the credit.

~

$\mathcal{F}$aith shines brightest in the dark.

Gettin' Old & Gettin' Good

Son Jimmy Varallo takes a big bite of chili at Varallo's 75th Anniversary celebration in October, 1982.

$\mathcal{G}$od didn't call them the ten suggestions.

~

$\mathcal{I}$f you aren't as close to God as you used to
be, guess who moved?

~

$\mathcal{C}$all on God, but row away from the rocks.

~

$\mathcal{G}$od provides food for the birds, but He
doesn't plant it in their nests.

Gettin' Old & Gettin' Good

Pray not for lighter burdens but for stronger backs.

⌐

When you come to the edge of all the light you have, step out on faith. You will either step onto something solid, or God will teach you how to fly.

⌐

Prayer is the outlet of sorrow and the inlet of solace and comfort.

⌐

God tells us to burden Him with whatever burdens us.

Thoughts from the Bottom of a Chili Bowl

Sorry looks back,
worried looks
around, faith
looks up.

Gettin' Old & Gettin' Good

167

*T*here is no saint without a past, no sinner
without a future.

❧

*L*ove in return for love is natural. Love in
return for hate is supernatural.

❧

*I*f you believe something, then you will live it.
If you don't live it, then you don't really
believe it.

❧

*I*f you are running from temptation, don't
leave a forwarding address.

Thoughts from the Bottom of a Chili Bowl

$\mathcal{G}$od's light knows no power shortage.

~

If you can think of nothing to give thanks for,
then you have a short memory.

~

$\mathcal{S}$ome people boast of being self-made; that
relieves God of a great responsibility.

~

$\mathcal{W}$here there is no faith in the future there is
no power in the present.

Gettin' Old & Gettin' Good

$\mathscr{D}$on't knock your church; things may have changed since you were there last.

~

$\mathscr{G}$od's delays are not God's denials.

Thoughts from the Bottom of a Chili Bowl

Don't wait till you get to heaven to act like an angel.

Gettin' Old & Gettin' Good

Grandsons Tony (l) and Todd (r) will be the third generation of Varallo's to serve chili at 817 Church Street

Mr. Frank and Mrs. Eva in front of the restaurant today

The front cover photograph was made in 1916 at the restaurant's first location—813 Church Street. Varallo's Restaurant has been in the 800 block of Church Street, Nashville, Tennessee for 78 years. Pictured are Frank Varallo, Sr., Joseph Zanini (brother-in-law), and James Daniels (employee).